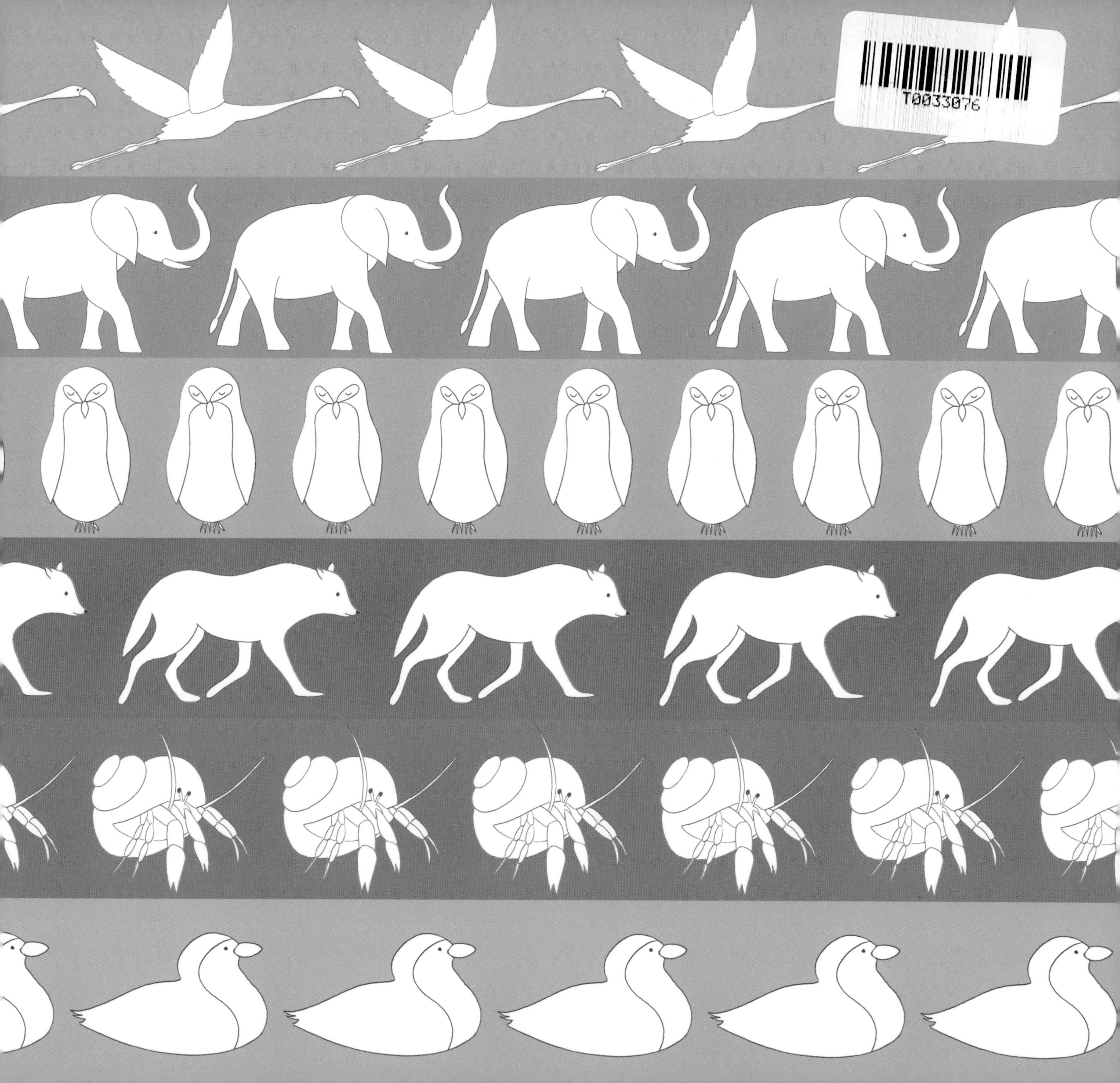
T0033076

For children who line up
everywhere

LINE UP!

ANIMALS IN REMARKABLE ROWS

WRITTEN AND ILLUSTRATED BY
SUSAN STOCKDALE

PEACHTREE
ATLANTA

Have you ever been asked
to line up in a row?

Some animals do this
when they're on the go!

Line up, elephant,
in a dusty gray train.

Then amble along
on the African plain.

Line up, spotted puffer,
so work can begin.

Striped fishes will clean
every part of your skin.

Line up, Arctic wolf,
on a cold, snowy day.

The paw tracks before you
will show you the way.

Line up, pink flamingo,
and rise from the lake.

The bird right behind you
will fly in your wake.

Line up, tired turtle,
and rest on a back.

Cozy up close
while you're propped in a stack.

Line up, little shrew,
and latch on to a tail.

Then scamper along
in an orderly trail.

Line up, hermit crab,
to select your new shell.

The one right before you
may fit very well.

Line up, tiny ant,
to crawl up a stalk.

The scent of your leader
will guide your steep walk.

Line up, Chinstrap Penguin,
to dive for small krill.

Then feast on the critters
you trap in your bill.

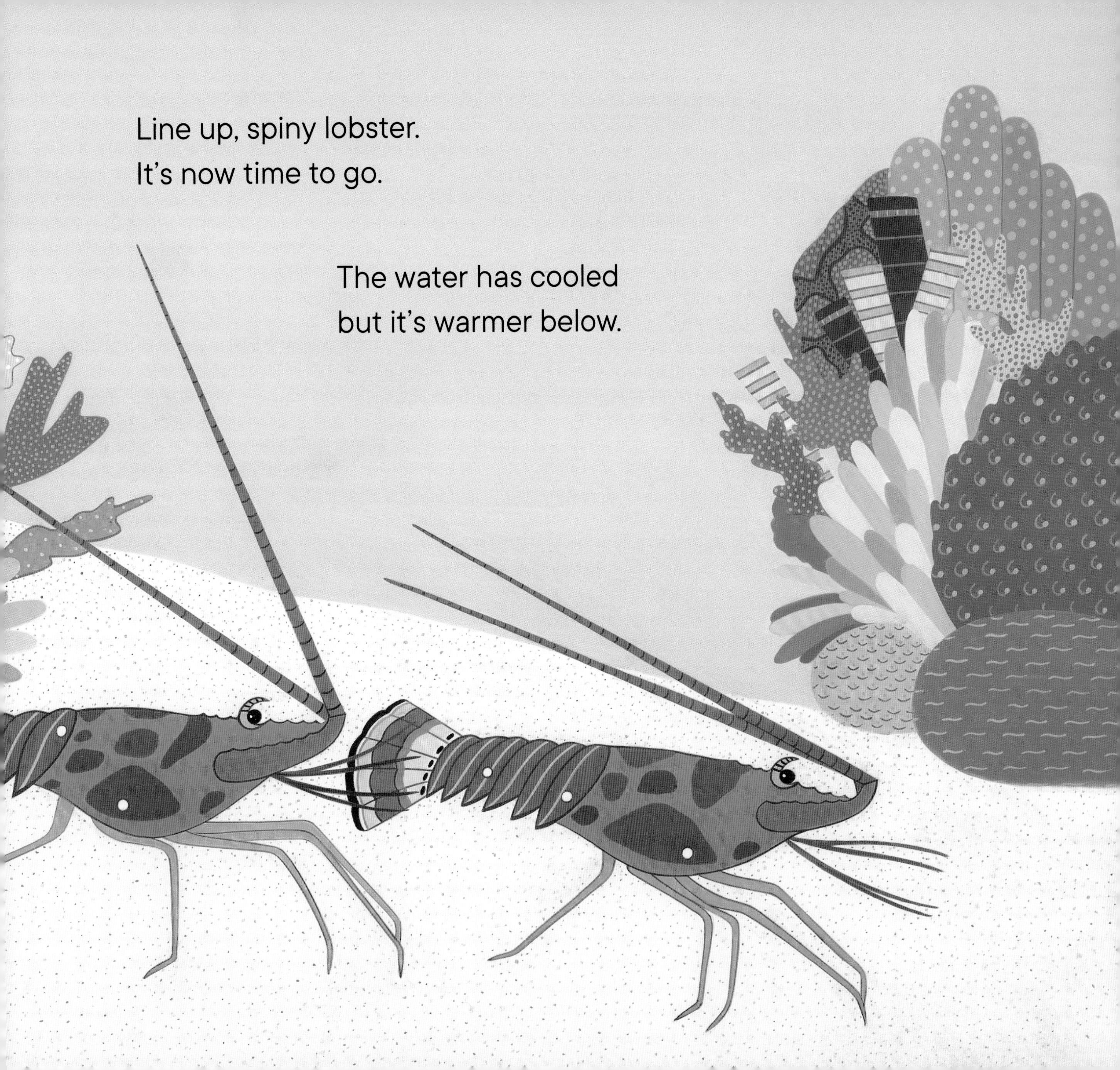

Line up, spiny lobster.
It's now time to go.

The water has cooled
but it's warmer below.

Line up, Fairywren.
Grab a branch and hold tight.

Then sleep standing up
as you nestle all night.

Stay warm, dozing creatures.

Sweet dreams, bedtime readers.

Good night.

Mallard

A newly hatched **Mallard duckling** stays close to its mother for safety, often following behind her and its siblings in a single file. The mother leads all her chicks to water within a day of hatching so they can take their first swim.

Bird; worldwide distribution, both native and introduced

African elephant

Led by the eldest female, called the matriarch, the members of an **African elephant** herd usually walk in an orderly line in search of food and water. The African elephant is the largest land mammal on earth.

Mammal; Africa

White-spotted pufferfish

Like many coral reef animals, a **White-spotted pufferfish** waits in line to have small cleaner fishes remove and eat harmful parasites and dead tissue from its skin. The pufferfish gets free skin care while the cleaners receive a free meal!

Fish; Indo-Pacific Ocean to the eastern Pacific Ocean

Arctic wolf

The **Arctic wolf** at the front of a pack creates a trail of slightly compacted snow for those behind it. This path makes it easier for other wolves to follow and prevents them from wasting vital energy.

Mammal; Arctic regions of North America and Greenland

American Flamingo

A flock of **American Flamingos** flies in a line, one slightly behind another, in order to lessen wind resistance, thereby conserving energy. Flamingos flock for safety, making it harder for a predator to pick out a single bird.

Bird; Caribbean Sea, the northern coast of South America, and the Galápagos Islands

Northern Map Turtle

Northern Map Turtles climb on top of one another so that each can get a better share of the sun's rays. The heat of the sun helps the turtles make Vitamin D, which is vital to their health.

Reptile; North America

North American least shrew

The mother **North American least shrew** directs her babies to form a train, known as a caravan, to keep them together. She heads the line, and each baby grasps the base of the tail of the shrew in front of it.

Mammal; North and Central America

Hermit crab

Hermit crabs use abandoned seashells as their home. When an empty shell washes up on shore, some hermit crabs line up according to size and swap shells in an orderly fashion.

Crustacean; Pacific, Atlantic, Indian, Arctic, and Southern oceans

Ant

An **ant** leader leaves a trail of pheromones—a chemical scent—to communicate with others. The other ants follow the trail to a food source or nest site or to avoid danger.

Insect; all continents except Antarctica and certain islands including Greenland and Iceland

Chinstrap Penguin

Chinstrap Penguins often walk in a row on the same straight path to the ocean to hunt for krill, small fish, and squid. A penguin has no teeth; instead it uses stiff spines on its tongue and the roof of its strong bill to catch and hold wiggling prey.

Bird; Antarctic region

Spiny lobster

The **Spiny lobster** prefers warm water. When shallow water begins to cool in autumn, the lobster migrates in a long, single file known as a queue to deeper, warmer water. It walks day and night in a group of up to fifty lobsters until it reaches its destination.

Crustacean; tropical and subtropical waters of the Atlantic Ocean and Caribbean Sea, extending into the Gulf of Mexico

Superb Fairywren

Superb Fairywrens roost closely together to share body heat and survive lower nighttime temperatures. Much like other perching birds, a Fairywren's feet automatically lock around a branch when its legs bend so it doesn't fall out of the tree while sleeping.

Bird; Australia

Acknowledgments

I am grateful to the following scientists at the Smithsonian Institution's National Museum of Natural History for their helpful research assistance: Dr. Sean Brady, Department of Entomology; Dr. Allen Collins, Department of Invertebrate Zoology; and Dr. Carla Dove, Dr. Louise Emmons, Dr. Melissa Hawkins, Diane Pitassy, and Dr. Kevin de Queiroz, Department of Vertebrate Zoology.

Published by
PEACHTREE PUBLISHING COMPANY INC.
1700 Chattahoochee Avenue
Atlanta, Georgia 30318-2112
PeachtreeBooks.com

Edited by Kathy Landwehr
Design and composition by Adela Pons
The illustrations were created in acrylic on paper.

On the front cover: hermit crab
On the back cover: American Flamingo

Printed and bound in August 2022 at Toppan Leefung, DongGuan, China.
10 9 8 7 6 5 4 3 2 1
First Edition
ISBN: 978-1-68263-322-9

Cataloging-in-Publication Data is available from the Library of Congress.

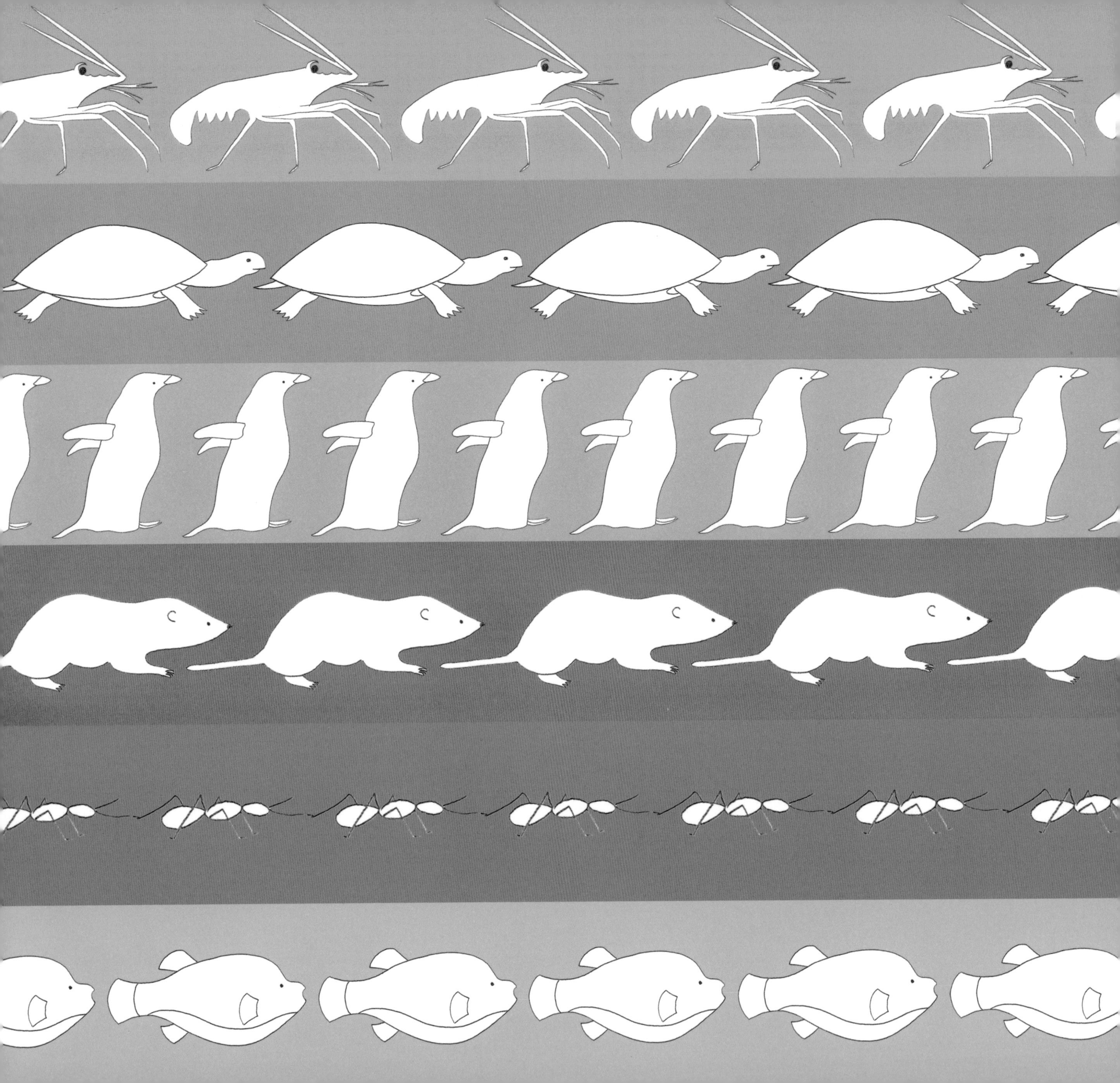